Margaret Miller

HOT OFF THE PRESS!

A Day at the

DAILY⊙NEWS

Introduction by James Hoge

CROWN PUBLISHERS, INC.
New York

Library of Congress Cataloging in Publication Data
Miller, Margaret. Hot off the press!.
Summary: Text and photographs describe a typical day at the Daily News from the gathering of the news, through the editing and printing, to the delivery of the completed newspaper.
1. Newspapers—Juvenile literature. 2. Daily news (New York, N.Y. : 1920)—Juvenile literature. [1. Newspapers. 2. Daily news (New York, N.Y. : 1920)] I. Daily news (New York, N.Y.: 1920) II. Title.   PN4776.M54 1985   070   85-4155
ISBN 0-517- 55647-2
Book design by Alan Benjamin
10 9 8 7 6 5 4 3 2 1
First Edition

ACKNOWLEDGMENTS

This book would not have been possible without the cooperation of the staff of the New York *Daily News*. Their good humor, courtesy, and patience were a pleasure. I not only want to thank all the people who are mentioned by name in this book but also the many more who are not. They were always willing to answer "one more question": Jay Aberbach, Bob Badolato, Al Bruno, Frank Cholewa, Ben Eisler, Rodrick Eyer, Marc Grossberg, Harry Helmstadt, Bill Kadian, Jack Kane, Norman Kaplan, Dennis Kemp, Kevin Lawler, Pat Luminello, Jerry Minogue, Ron Monje, Liz Rittersporn, Joe Russo, Keith Torrie, and Warren Welch.

I am especially grateful to James Hoge, Publisher, for his continued support, and to Bob Lane, Assistant to the Editor, for his exceptional help and guidance.

My thanks also to Kate, Jacob, and Alan Reuther; Michael and Jocelyn Simonson; and Beth Lief for their help in this project.

Last, I want to thank Alan Benjamin for the splendid idea and design of this book; and Ann Tobias and Thea Feldman for their excellent criticism and advice.

Photo on page 28 courtesy of the *Daily News*

For David,
for his encouragement, support,
and love

Introduction

People like to be informed about the news of their neighborhoods, their towns and cities, their country, and the world. One of the best ways to keep up with the news is to read a newspaper. While large numbers of people read newspapers, only a surprisingly small number know how a newspaper is produced. News must be gathered, written, photographed, and printed. After that, newspapers must be cut to size, folded, and delivered to readers. How is all this done?

It is not a simple task. There are many different steps involved. By following how one newspaper, the New York *Daily News,* turns a specific event, the Macy's Annual Thanksgiving Day Parade, into a story, readers will see these steps taking place and come away from this book with an understanding of the newspaper publishing process.

The New York *Daily News* is read each day by millions of people. The goal of the *Daily News* is to publish the news of each day about New York City, America, and the world. Everyone who works at the *Daily News* wants the stories in the newspaper to state not only the important facts, but to be interesting and easy to read.

Many people doing different jobs come together to bring out the New York *Daily News*. This book describes who they are, and how they do their jobs. All of them work hard and are proud of what they do. By knowing how this newspaper is published, it is my hope that the readers of *Hot Off the Press!* will enjoy their own newspapers even more, whether they read small, country journals or large, city dailies.

James Hoge,
Publisher,
New York *Daily News*

It is a cold Thanksgiving Day morning in New York City. In the *Daily News* Building on the East Side of the city, men and women are working on tomorrow's newspaper.

On the city's West Side, the balloons, floats, marching bands, and clowns in the Macy's Annual Thanksgiving Day Parade have been gathering since the middle of the night. Today's parade is a major news story for tomorrow's *Daily News*.

The offices of the *Daily News* are open twenty-four hours a day, every day of the week, because somewhere in the world news is always happening. Each day the *Daily News* is brand new. It may include stories based on local events, such as the Thanksgiving Day Parade, or news from far away, such as the story of an earthquake on the other side of the world.

In ten hours all the ingredients for each morning's newspaper—news stories, photographs, sports, movie and book reviews, fashion, comics, TV listings, and advertisements—must be written, pho-tographed, edited, and put together like a complicated jigsaw puzzle.

The City Room is the heart of the *Daily News*. In this enormous room, crowded with desks, the reporters, editors, and artists work closely with one another. A large clock hangs from the ceiling in the middle of the room. Everyone watches the time closely, because strict deadlines must be met throughout the day.

The City Desk is in the City Room. There the City Editor, Bob Herbert, decides which local events are newsworthy and assigns reporters to write stories about them.

At 8:10 on Thanksgiving morning, Bob talks with two reporters, Suzanne Golubski and Jim Harney, about the Thanksgiving Day Parade. Bob tells Suzanne and Jim the kind of story he wants. "Look for colorful details. Talk with marchers in the parade, the spectators, and the police. This parade happens every year, so try to find ways to make this story different from the one written last year."

Paul says, "I want dramatic shots of the balloons as they come down the street between the buildings. Pick out a good spot and hold on to it. Get lots of crowd shots, especially ones of the kids all bundled up."

The Photo Assignment Desk is covered with telephones and police radios. The photographers carry walkie-talkies so that they can communicate with the Photo Assignment Editors and with one another while they are on the job.

A few feet from the City Desk is the Photo Assignment Desk. Paul DeMaria, the Photo Assignment Editor, and Tom Monaster, a *Daily News* photographer, look at the photographs of last year's parade. Tom is one of three *News* photographers who will take pictures of today's parade.

While Paul and Tom are talking about the parade, a call comes in over the police radio about a warehouse fire. Assistant Editor Willie Anderson talks into two phones at once as he quickly locates a photographer and sends him to the scene.

By 8:45 A.M. Tom and Suzanne have reached their assigned positions on the parade route. There are reporters and photographers covering the parade for all the New York City newspapers, as well as for the Associated Press (AP) and United Press International (UPI).

AP and UPI maintain offices throughout the world. The reporters and photographers who work for these companies supply a major portion of the news stories and photographs that appear in newspapers all over the country. AP and UPI are often referred to as "wire services." The name comes from the days when stories were tapped out in Morse code on telegraph wires. Today AP and UPI stories come through the telephone lines directly into the computer terminals in the *News* City Room. Wire service photographs are reproduced in a few minutes on special photo machines.

At 9:00 A.M. the Macy's Annual Thanksgiving Day Parade begins. In the midst of the large crowds, Suzanne and Tom start to work.

As Suzanne talks with the spectators each one responds openly. She puts people at ease while writing their names in her notebook. She also records what they say and what she sees. Suzanne is skilled at both asking questions and listening to answers.

Tom's two cameras, camera bag, and walkie-talkie are a heavy load, but he moves swiftly in the street looking for different viewpoints for his photographs. He is accustomed to working quickly and under difficult circumstances. Tom will take almost 150 photographs because, as Paul DeMaria says, "You can always rewrite a story but you can't rewrite a picture."

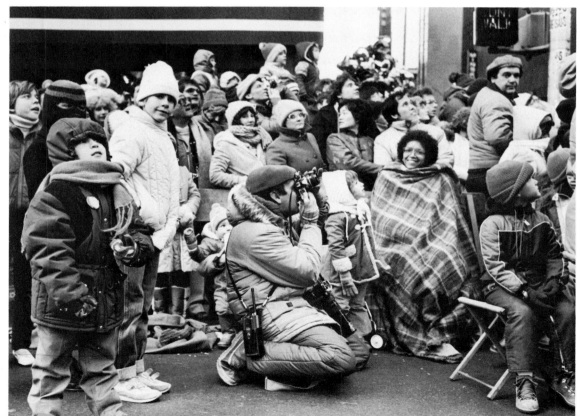

By 12:30 P.M. the chilled reporters and photographers have returned to the offices of the *Daily News*. Suzanne and Jim meet with Don Singleton in the City Room. Don is a "rewrite man," a writer who has a talent for using the notes of other reporters and writing a story in very little time. A news story should answer six basic questions: who, what, where, when, why, and how.

Listening to the reporters, Don types on a keyboard directly into a computer. A video terminal, similar to a TV screen, displays Don's story.

"I realize that I have ten times as much good stuff as I can use," Don explains. "I have to sort through all the material and put together in a hour a good parade story that is not just straight facts. We also want the story filled with the atmosphere of the parade—the cold, sunny day and the crowds."

Don's finished story is stored on a memory disk in the computer with an identifying title called a "slug." The slug for his story is "Parade/23." The "23" refers to the date of tomorrow's newspaper, Friday, November 23.

At 2:00 P.M. City Editor Bob Herbert types "Parade/23" on his keyboard to call up the story on his terminal so that he and Don can read it together. All stories that Bob has assigned must meet with his approval.

At the Copy Desk, located at the far end of the City Room, the head Copy Editor, Len Valenti, calls up the parade story on the computer after Bob has approved it. Len is called the slotman because he sits in the middle, or slot, of a U-shaped desk while the other copy editors sit around the outside. The slotman assigns Sally Blanchard the story.

After Sally has carefully checked the parade story for accuracy in spelling, grammar, and punctuation, her next job is to write the headline. A headline must tell the reader what the story is about, and it must fit into the available space.

In very little time Sally selects the words, "All Puffed Up for Thanksgiving," for the main headline that runs the width of the page. When Sally and Len are satisfied with the story and the headline, Sally punches the "type set" button on her keyboard.

At the same time that Suzanne, Jim, and Don are working on the parade story in the City Room, the photographers deliver their film to the *News* Photo Lab where it is developed in a few minutes by automated machines.

Then Phil Stanziola, the Photo Lab Manager, searches through the developed film for the most dramatic shots of balloons, floats, and crowds. From more than 700 negatives Phil selects 62 for the darkroom to print. The finished prints are sent through a pneumatic tube to the Photo Desk in the City Room.

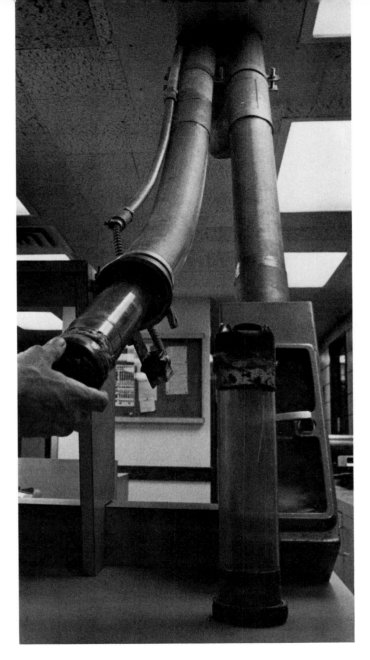

Jim discusses the front-page photograph with the Managing Editor, Jim Willse. The Managing Editor is in charge of the overall, day-to-day operation of the newspaper. Jim Willse picks out a dramatic AP photograph of Underdog, one of the giant balloons, nose-diving to the street. He says, "This is the best picture. Nothing is going to beat this one. Let's run it on page one."

At 2:00 in the afternoon Jim Garrett, the Photo Editor, sits at the Photo Desk surrounded by the sixty-two parade photographs. Jim must select photographs for three places in tomorrow's paper: the front page; the parade story, which appears inside the newspaper; and the "double truck," which is the centerfold or middle two pages of the *News*.

A velox is a print composed of tiny, solid black dots that vary in size. With a magnifying glass, this dot pattern is easily visible in photographs in a newspaper. A velox machine delivers a print of the Raggedy Ann balloon to Roy Lake.

In the Art Department Bill Robinson touches up the selected parade photographs with special paints so that they will print more clearly in the newspaper. Bill then sends the prints through the pneumatic tube to the Photo Engraving Department, where they are photographed again and printed as veloxes.

DAILY EDITION	ART DEPARTMENT	NATIONAL & CITY DESK	NEWS DESK	SPORTS & COPY DESK	COMPOSING ROOM CLOSE	PRESS START
National	4:30 P.M.	5:00 P.M.	5:30 P.M.	5:45 P.M.	6:15 P.M.	7:30 P.M.
3-Star	7:15 P.M.	7:45 P.M.	8:05 P.M.	8:25 P.M.	8:45 P.M.	10:00 P.M.
4-Star	9:45 P.M.	10:10 P.M.	10:25 P.M.	10:45 P.M.	11:00 P.M.	11:45 P.M.
Racing Final	11:45 P.M.	Midnight	12:20 A.M.	12:45 A.M.	1:00 A.M.	1:30 A.M.
Sports Final	1:00 A.M.	1:25 A.M.	1:40 A.M.	1:55 A.M.	2:15 A.M.	3:00 A.M.

By 4:30 in the afternoon the pace in the City Room is hurried and hectic. Everyone is rushing to meet the 5:30 deadline for the early edition. The *News* publishes five separate editions of the paper during the night. Each edition has its own set of deadlines. The layout of the paper will be changed for each edition to include late-breaking news stories as well as the results of evening sporting events.

Joe Kovach, the News Editor, decides where to place the news stories throughout the paper. The important articles, those that interest and affect the most people, appear on the opening pages. Joe decides to place the parade story on page three.

The first five pages of the *Daily News* are called "open" pages and are devoted solely to news. From page six on, Joe lays out the stories around the advertisements. He works with "the Book," which are layout pages prepared every day by the *News* Advertising Department. The Book shows the position of the ads on each page of the newspaper.

After the News Editor has decided which stories will be in tomorrow's newspaper, printing plates must be made. Plates are used to print multiple copies of a newspaper. Until five years ago these printing plates were made of lead at the *Daily News*. The type for the words was also made of lead by seventy linotype machines. Today, these printing plates are made of cardboard, and four computer typesetters, called Merganthaler 606's, photographically print all the type for the *Daily News* onto glossy white paper.

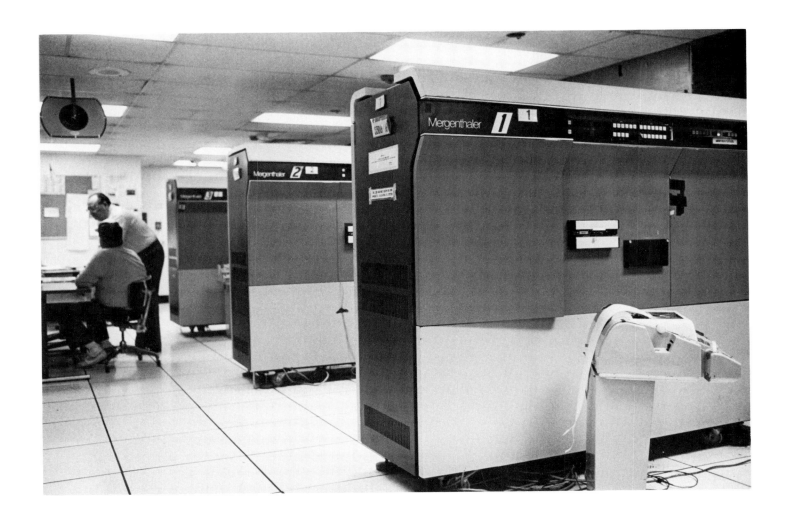

Inside a Merganthaler 606 a beam of light projects each letter of each word in the newspaper onto light-sensitive photographic paper at an incredible speed.

The 606 is capable of making 3,000 letters per minute. If the 606 were, for example, to make the type for this book, it would take less than four minutes.

At 5:30 P.M. Mickey Gebo receives the steady stream of type that is coming out of the 606's into the Composing Room. Here compositors paste down the type and the photographs onto 132 sheets of lightweight, white cardboard, called "boards," one for each page of tomorrow's newspaper.

Another compositor has pasted down the headlines, photographs, and captions on the centerfold.

Bert Eldridge is the front page compositor. A layout sheet shows him the position of the headlines and the photograph for the parade story. Using a razor, Bert carefully cuts the type and the velox of Underdog to the right size before gluing each piece in its correct place on the board.

By 6:15 P.M. all 132 boards for the early edition, including the parade story on page three and the parade photographs on the centerfold, have been pasted down and filed in wooden slots in the Control Section until they are needed.

The *Daily News* owns three printing plants. Each one is over an hour's drive from the *Daily News* Building. Instead of delivering the completed boards to each plant, a Laser Reader rapidly transmits all the pages of the *News* to each printing plant.

In the Laser Room of the printing plant, Henry Lee removes a negative from a Laser Writer. A Laser Writer is programmed to make negatives from the pages sent by the Reader.

Ken Johnson feeds the boards into the Laser Reader. Inside the Reader, a red beam of laser light, which makes 6,000 revolutions per minute, scans the pasted-up boards and converts the copy into electronic impulses. In two and one half minutes the Reader will send the material on four boards by microwave from an antenna on the roof of the *News* building to the plants.

In a negative the colors are reversed: the areas that will print black are clear, and the areas that will be white in the finished newspaper are black.

As each negative is received in the Laser Room, it is passed into the Plate-making Room. There a thin layer of liquid plastic is laid down on a sheet of lightweight cardboard. Mike Hachikian places the negative in the platemaking machine. Then an ultraviolet, high-intensity light shines through the negative onto the liquid plastic.

The light penetrates the clear areas of the negative and hardens the plastic. In the black areas of the negative, which will become the white areas of the newspaper, the light does not reach the plastic, and therefore it does not harden. The liquid plastic that remains is blown away by tiny jets of air. Finally, a cloth sweeps across the hardened plate, blotting up any excess plastic. A lightweight, flexible printing plate with raised type and photographs has been produced.

Each night vast quantities of paper and ink are used to print more than 1,700,000 copies of the *Daily News*. The three printing plants use approximately 2,641 gallons of ink—enough to fill a small swimming pool—and 625 rolls of paper, called "newsprint." A full roll of newsprint weighs 1,800 pounds. Each roll is 5 feet wide and over 6½ miles long.

The basement floors of the printing plants are filled with equipment to handle the enormous rolls of newsprint. Trucks deliver newsprint throughout the

night. The rolls come off the truck with a thundering noise and land on a conveyor belt. The conveyor belt carries the rolls to a storage room where they are pushed into neat rows. When newsprint is needed in the Press Room, the huge rolls are moved there by a man-powered mini-railroad system.

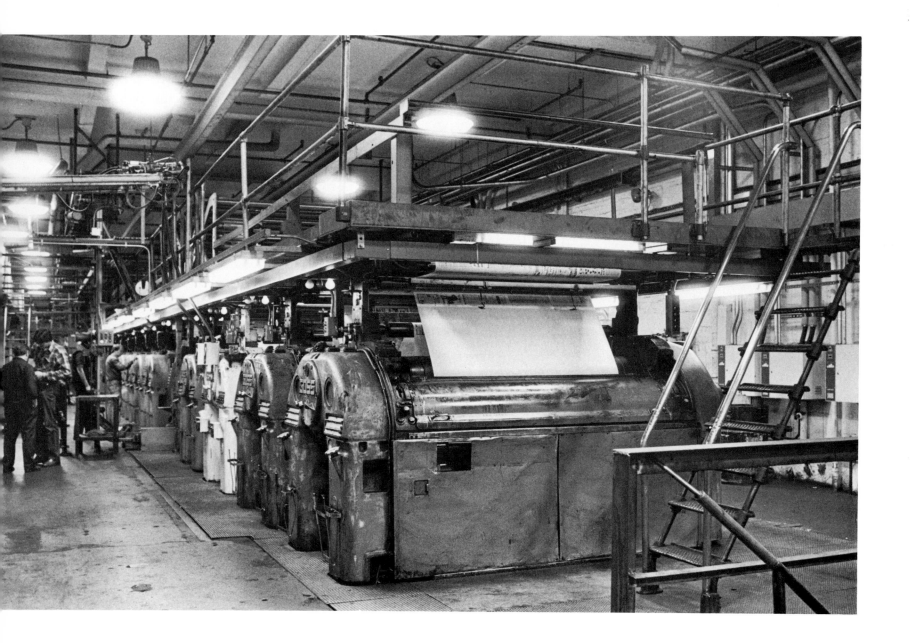

At 7:00 P.M. the pressmen prepare to print the first edition. Newspaper printing presses are enormous machines that can turn newsprint into a finished newspaper in less than three minutes. Each press can print over 50,000 newspapers an hour.

When the presses are running, the building vibrates with noise. The roar of the machinery is so loud that it is impossible to hear another person talk, even if he is yelling. To protect their hearing, the pressmen are required to wear earplugs.

The presses stand two stories high. The lower floor of the Press Room is called the "Reel Room," where the rolls of newsprint are loaded onto the presses.

Jack Feldmann and Calvin Weeks push a roll of newsprint onto a small metal wagon that moves on tracks between the presses. They ease the roll into position and lock it into place. When the roll runs out, another roll automatically replaces it.

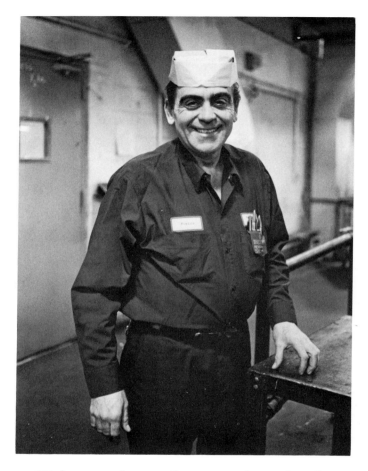

Using a piece of newsprint, the foreman of the Press Room, Vito Piazza, folds his paper hat. These hats, traditionally worn by pressmen, are practical protection against dripping ink.

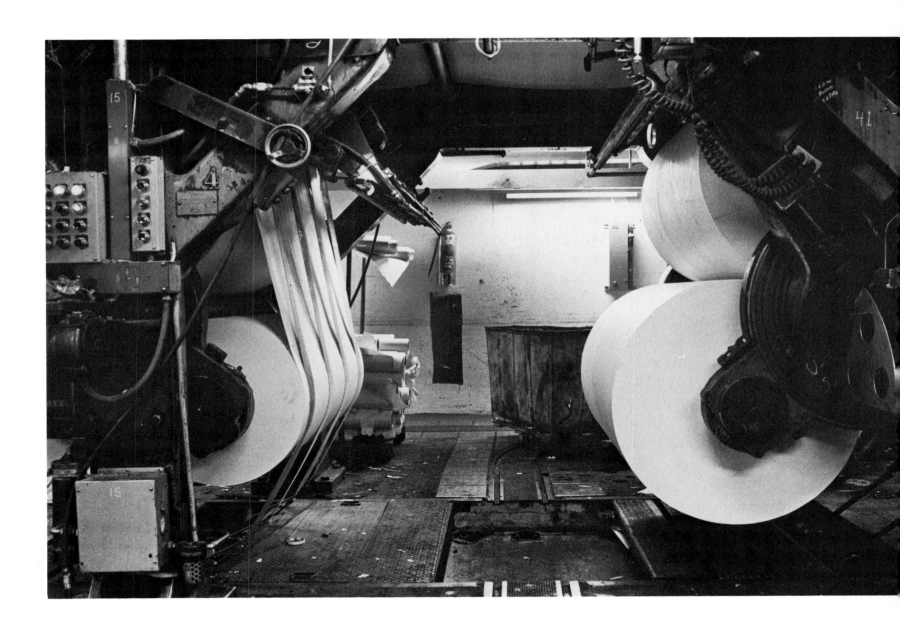

The upper floor of the Press Room is where the newspapers are printed, cut, and folded. Tony Garretto fits a printing plate into position on the printing cylinder.

This method of printing is called "letterpress." Like a simple rubber stamp, the raised areas of the printing plates are inked and then pressed against the newsprint, leaving a printed impression of the newspaper pages.

The presses start printing at 7:30 each night. The newsprint, which moves at twenty miles per hour, is a blur.

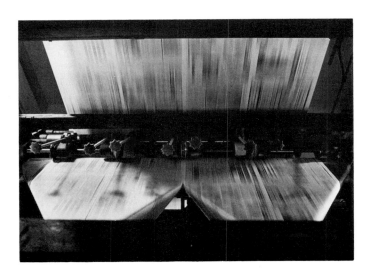

Jim Ryan, the Press Room Superintendent, and Vito Corcione, a pressman, constantly check the newspapers to make sure the printing quality is high and the newspapers are clear and readable. Above the presses, the finished newspapers are taken by conveyor belts to the Mail Room.

After the paper is printed, the presses feed continuous sheets of newsprint into machines that cut, fold, and combine the pages in order. The completed newspapers are then carried on a vertical conveyor belt, called a "stream," to the top of the Press Room.

By 7:35 P.M. on Thanksgiving Day, November 22, the first copies of the Friday, November 23, *Daily News* have dropped from the conveyor belt into the counting and stacking machine in the Mail Room. Stacks of fifty papers then pass through a tying machine where they are wrapped with thin nylon cord.

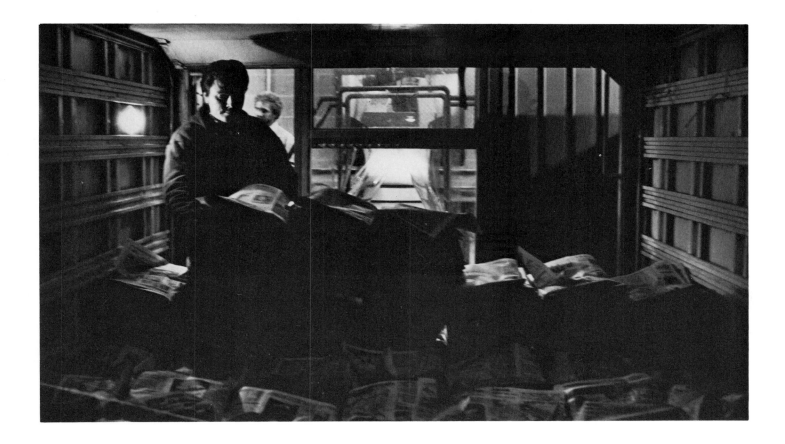

Outside, the parking lot is filled with *Daily News* delivery trucks. One by one, they back up to the Mail Room doors.

Ken Anderson, a driver, picks up the tied bundles from a conveyor belt and loads them into the back of his truck. In the next four hours, Ken will make 100 stops to deliver the *Daily News* to stores and newsstands throughout New York City.

Tomorrow morning the people of New York will read about the events of the day before, beginning with the Macy's Annual Thanksgiving Day Parade.